The International System of Units (SI) - Conversion Factors for General Use

Editors:

Kenneth S. Butcher
Linda D. Crown
Elizabeth J. Gentry
Weights and Measures Division

Carol Hockert, Chief
Weights and Measures Division
Technology Services
National Institute of Standards and Technology

May 2006

U.S. Department of Commerce
Carlo M. Gutierrez, Secretary

Technology Administration
*Robert Cresanti, Under Secretary
of Commerce for Technology*

**National Institute of
Standards and Technology**
William Jeffrey, Director

Certain commercial entities, equipment, or materials may be identified in this document in order to describe an experimental procedure or concept adequately. Such identification is not intended to imply recommendation or endorsement by the National Institute of Standards and Technology, nor is it intended to imply that the entities, materials, or equipment are necessarily the best available for the purpose.

TABLE OF CONTENTS

FOREWORD

This publication lists the units of the International System of Units (SI), or metric system, recommended for use in trade and commerce and other general uses by the National Institute of Standards and Technology.

Please submit comments or suggestions to the Editor at:

Elizabeth J. Gentry
National Institute of Standards and Technology
Weights and Measures Division
100 Bureau Drive, Stop 2600
Gaithersburg, Maryland 20899-2600

E-mail: *TheSI@nist.gov*

Visit our Website at: http://www.nist.gov/metric

For information on scientific units go to: http://physics.nist.gov/cuu/Units/index.html

Telephone: 301-975-3690   FAX: 301-926-0647

1   SCOPE

In 1988 Congress designated the International System of Units (SI), the metric system, as the preferred system of measurement for use in trade and commerce (15 U.S.C. §205 – 267). This publication provides guidance on the use of the International System of Units (SI) to ensure uniformity with the weights and measures usage in the commercial measurement system and in other applications. Government and industry use metric units for [1]procurements, grants and other business-related activities, for educational information, and for guidance in publications. The practical guidance in this publication may be used for, but is not limited to, the drafting of laws, regulations, contracts, product specifications, purchase orders, and the preparation of public information, reports and brochures, correspondence, statistical tables, databases, and maps. In addition to serving as an authoritative document for the conversion of customary[2] (inch-pound) units to metric, this publication also explains the relationship between metric units and inch-pound units.

2   REFERENCE DOCUMENTS

This publication is based on *National Institute of Standards and Technology (NIST) SP 330 – International System of Units (SI) (2001)(http://physics.nist.gov/Pubs/SP330/contents.html), NIST SP 811 – Guide for the Use of the International System of Units (SI)(1995)(http://physics.nist.gov/Pubs/SP811/cover.html), NIST 814 – Interpretation of the SI for the United States and Metric Conversion Policy for Federal Agencies (1998) (http://ts.nist.gov/ts/htdocs/200/202/pub814.htm), and the IEEE/ASTM SI 10^{TM} American National Standard for Use of the International System of Units (SI): The Modern Metric System (2002),* developed by the Institute of Electrical and Electronics Engineers, Inc., and the American Society for Testing and Materials (ASTM) International and other selected publications noted in Section 6

3   DEFINITIONS

3.1   SI Units

Units belonging to the International System of Units (SI), as interpreted or modified for use in the United States by the Secretary of Commerce through the National Institute of Standards and Technology may be used in trade and commerce, procurements, grants and other business-related activities, in educational information, and as guidance in publications to increase understanding of the metric system.

3.2   Inch-Pound Units

Units based upon the inch, pound, and gallon were historically derived from the English system and subsequently were re-defined as multiples of SI Units in U.S. law beginning in 1893. For example, the inch is defined as the length corresponding to 2.54 centimeters (exactly); and the gallon is defined as the volume corresponding to 3.785412 liters; in other words, the inch-pound (customary) units are based on the SI units and multiplication or division is used to convert units from one system to another.

For example, since the inch was defined as the length corresponding to 2.54 centimeters, in order to convert inches to centimeters multiply the value to be converted by 2.54. An extensive set of conversion factors between the two systems of units is listed in Section 5. In this document, the term inch-pound unit includes the degree Fahrenheit. Some inch-pound units, such as the gallon, have the same name as units previously used in other countries but differ in magnitude. When the term gallon is used, it means a U.S. gallon of 128 fluid ounces (231 cubic inches).

---

[1]   Vol. 63 F.R. No. 144; Page 40334, July 28, 1998, reprinted in NIST SP 814
[2]   Throughout this document the terms **customary** and **inch-pound** units will be used interchangeably.

4 GENERAL REQUIREMENTS

4.1 Preferred SI (metric) Units

The SI units preferred for use are the units (together with their multiples and submultiples).

4.1.1 SI Base Units

The SI is constructed from seven base units, which are adequate to describe most of the measurements used in science, industry and commerce.

Quantity	Unit Name	Symbol
length	meter	m
mass[3]	kilogram	kg
time	second	s
electric current	ampere	A
thermodynamic temperature	kelvin	K
amount of substance	mole	mol
luminous intensity	candela	cd

Table 1. The SI Base Units.

4.1.2 SI Derived Units

Derived units are formed for convenience of notation and are mainly used by various branches of science. They are obtained by combining base units and other derived units algebraically. The symbols for derived units are obtained by means of the mathematical signs for multiplication, division, and use of exponents. For example, the SI unit for velocity is the *meter per second* (m/s or m • s^{-1}), and that for angular velocity is the *radian per second* (rad/s or rad • s^{-1}). Some derived SI units have special names and symbols. Almost all physical measurements of science, industry and trade can be expressed in terms of these units or other combinations. For convenience, however, other units can be derived from these, such as the hectare (ha) for an area of land or the liter (L or l) for volume, plus others (with symbols of their own) such as pressure (pascal) or electric resistance (ohm).

4.1.3 SI Prefixes

The units often have **prefixes**, indicating the power(s) of 10 by which a unit may be multiplied (for example, the prefix <u>kilo</u> in kilometer indicates that the unit kilometer is 1000 times larger than the meter). They are attached to an SI unit name or symbol to form what are properly called "multiples" and "submultiples" (i.e., positive or negative powers of 10) of the SI unit. These prefixes are helpful when referring to very small or very large quantities. Instead of creating a new unit, a prefix is added. For example, when measuring short lengths such as 1/1000th of a meter, we simply write **milli**meter; milli denotes 1/1000 th.

---

[3] In commercial and everyday use, and in many technical fields, the term "weight" is usually used as a synonym for mass. This is how "weight" is used in most United States laws and regulations. See the note in section 5.2.1 for further explanation.

The common metric prefixes are:

Multiplication Factor	Prefix Name	Prefix Symbol
$1\ 000\ 000\ 000\ 000 = 10^{12}$	tera	T
$1\ 000\ 000\ 000 = 10^{9}$	giga	G
$1\ 000\ 000 = 10^{6}$	mega	M
$1\ 000 = 10^{3}$	kilo	k
$100 = 10^{2}$	hecto	h
$10 = 10^{1}$	deka	da
$0.1 = 10^{-1}$	deci	d
$0.01 = 10^{-2}$	centi	c
$0.001 = 10^{-3}$	milli	m
$0.000\ 001 = 10^{-6}$	micro	μ
$0.000\ 000\ 001 = 10^{-9}$	nano	n
$0.000\ 000\ 000\ 001 = 10^{-12}$	pico	p
This table shows the common prefixes. Others, from 10^{-24} to 10^{24} are acceptable for use of the SI. See NIST SP 330.		

Table 2. SI Prefixes.

Prefixes produce units that are of an appropriate size for the application, e.g., millimeter for measurement of the dimensions of small screws, or kilometer for the measurement of distances on maps. Examples that show reasonable choices of multiples and submultiples for many practical applications are given in Section 5. While all combinations are technically correct, many are not used in practice. The prefixes deci, deka, and hecto are rarely used; prefixes that are multiples or submultiples of 1000 are generally preferred. When the unit name is written in full, the prefix is written in full: megahertz, not Mhertz. When the unit symbol is used, the prefix symbol is used: MHz, not megaHz. Only one prefix should be used in forming a multiple of an SI unit, e.g., μV, not mmV. Prefix symbols for multiples of a million or greater are capitalized, and those for less than a million are written in lower case.

4.1.4 Editorial Style

The names of all SI units begin with a lower case letter except, of course, at the beginning of a sentence or when other grammar rules dictate capitalizing nouns. There is one exception: in "degree Celsius" the term "degree" is lower case but "Celsius" is always capitalized.

SI symbols are always written in lower case except for the liter and those units derived from the name of a person (e.g., W for Watt, Pa for Pascal, etc.).

SI symbols are unique—they are not abbreviations and should not be followed by a period (except at the end of a sentence). Likewise, symbols stand for both the singular and plural of the unit and should not have an "s" added when more than one.

SI units are always written in an upright typeface with a space between the numeric value and the symbol.[4]

SI symbols should not be used in a sentence to indicate the units they represent unless the symbol has a number preceding it (e.g., "the kilometer measures length" not "the km measures length.")

---

[4] A space is not required between the numeric value and SI symbols which appear in the net quantity of content declarations of packaged goods available in the commercial marketplace. For information on the labeling requirements for packaged goods sold in the commercial marketplace see the Uniform Packaging and Labeling Regulation in National Institute of Standards and Technology Handbook 130 "Uniform Laws and Regulations in the Field of Legal Metrology…" at *http//:www.nist.gov/metric* on the Internet.

4.2 Accepted Units

For practical reasons a number of non-metric units are accepted for use. These include units of time (minute, hour, etc.), units of plane angle (degree, etc.), and a few units for special applications, such as the nautical mile, used in navigation. Section 5 includes accepted units and shows their areas of application. These units may be used in full compliance with the provisions of the Metric Conversion Law (15 U.S.C. 205(a)), Executive Order 12770, and the Federal Register Notice, "Metric System of Measurement; Interpretation of the International System of Units for the United States" (63 F.R. 40334, July 28, 1998)[5].

4.3 Unacceptable Metric Units

Many older metric practices are no longer acceptable. Particular care shall be taken to avoid introducing non-SI practices into the United States in areas where such practices are not now established. The units listed in the subsections 4.3.1 and 4.3.2 shall not be used.

4.3.1 Centimeter-Gram-Second (CGS) Units

Units with special names peculiar to the various CGS metric systems shall not be used. Conversion factors are provided for some of these units to assist the users of this document in converting those values to SI units. Among these units are the following that have been commonly used:

CGS Units that Shall Not be Used	Typical Applications
erg, dyne, gal	used in mechanics
poise, stokes	used in fluid dynamics
stilb, phot, lambert	used in photometry
emu, esu, gauss, oersted, maxwell, gilbert, biot, franklin, abampere, abvolt, statvolt, etc.	used in electricity and magnetism

Table 3. CGS Units Not to be Used.

4.3.2 Deprecated Names or Symbols

Other units from older versions of the metric system, some terms not recommended for continued use, and jargon that shall not be used include:

Deprecated Term or Symbol	Correct Unit
kilo	kilogram
calorie	joule (J), if the value is used in physics kilojoule (kJ), if the value is used in nutrition
candle or candlepower	candela
centiliter	milliliter or liter
fermi	femtometer
gamma	nanotesla
micron	micrometer
millimicron	nanometer
mho	siemens
γ (gamma)	microgram
λ (lambda)	cubic millimeter or microliter

Table 4. Deprecated Names and Symbols.

---

[5]   See NIST Special Publication 814, 1998 edition.

4.3.3   Miscellaneous Non-SI Units Not to be Used

Additional units that are not accepted for use include the following:

ångström
g_n as a unit of acceleration (g_n= 9.806 65 ms^{-2})[6]
grade or gon [1 grade = (π/200) rad]
kilogram-force
langley (1 langley = 1 cal/cm^2)
metric carat (use carat, which is 200 mg)
metric horsepower
millimeter of mercury
millimeter, centimeter, or meter of water
standard atmosphere (101.325 kPa)
technical atmosphere (98.0665 kPa)
torr (133.322 Pa)

Table 5. Non-SI Units Not to be Used.

4.4   Conversion

Conversion is a multi-step process that involves multiplication or division by a numerical factor, selection of the correct number of significant digits[7], and rounding. The following sections are intended as a guide through this multi-step process.

Conversion factors in Section 5 are shown from inch-pound units to SI units, generally to seven significant digits. The first column, labeled **To Convert From**, lists inch-pound and other units commonly used to express the quantities; the second column, labeled **To**, gives SI units or other preferred units; and the third column, labeled **Multiply By**, gives the conversion factor by which the numerical value in **To Convert From** units must be multiplied to obtain the numerical value in **To** units.

If the inch-pound value is expressed by a combination of units such as feet and inches, or pounds and ounces, it should first be converted to the smaller unit.

Examples: 12 feet 5 inches = 149 inches
                 1 pound 3-1/2 ounces = 19.5 ounces

For conversion from inch-pound units to SI units, multiply by the factor given in Section 5. For example, to convert 10.1 feet to meters multiple by 0.3048:

10.1 feet x 0.3048 = 3.07848 m

At this point it is good practice to keep all of the digits, especially if other mathematical operations or conversions will follow. Rounding should be the last step of the conversion process and should be performed only once.

---

[6]   The acceleration due to gravity is a variable quantity rather than a unit. It may be used in multiples to express accelerations, such as 2.7g. It should be presented without a space between the coefficient and the quantity symbol, with the quantity symbol in slanted or italic type, and with no plural indications made by adding an "s." The value used in each document should be specified, even if the standard value g_n = 9.806 65 ms^{-2} is used.

[7]   The number of significant digits is the number of digits used to express a number. One or more leading zeroes are not treated as significant, e.g., 00 257.7 has 4 significant digits, and 0.004 92 has 3 significant digits. Trailing zeros located to the right of the decimal point are to be considered significant, however. Zeros with significant digits on each side are also significant. Thus 30.4, 34.0, and 3.40 each have three significant digits but 340 must be taken as having only two significant digits.

4.4.1 Rounding

Before attempting to round a converted number, it is important to establish the purpose of rounding and the application that it will be used in. If the converted values are being used to develop a technical document or a specification, round the converted number to maintain the precision of the measurement using the guidance provided in 4.4.1.1. When the purpose of the rounding is to provide equivalent units for use in general use documents or reports, simple rules of rounding in 4.4.1.2 are recommended. Additional guidance on rounding is available in Annex B of IEEE/ASTM Standard SI 10™ (2002) and NIST Special Publication 811 (1995).

Where an inch-pound unit represents a maximum or minimum limit (e.g., in a law or regulation), the rounding must be done in a direction where the metric value does not violate the original limit by increasing or decreasing it inappropriately. For example, for most applications 10 feet rounds to 3 meters, but if a safety code requires 10 feet of clearance from electrical lines, a converted value of 3.05 meters must be used until studies show that 3 meters of clearance is adequate.

If, however, the purpose of rounding involves a commercially available package, product, or commodity, the most appropriate procedure may be to round the converted value down for the reasons described in 4.4.1.2.

4.4.1.1 Rounding Procedure for Technical Documents or Specifications

The number of significant digits retained must be such that accuracy is neither sacrificed nor exaggerated. The first step of the rounding process is to establish the number of significant digits to be retained. In order to maintain the accuracy of the converted number, the following procedure[8] may be used:

(i) If the **first** significant digit of the converted value is **greater than or equal to** the **first** significant digit of the original value, round the converted value to the **same** number of significant digits as there are in the original value.

Examples: In converting 60.5 miles to kilometers, first multiply the inch-pound value by the conversion factor:

60.5 miles x 1.609347 = **97**.36549 km

The **first** significant digit of the metric value (9) is **greater than** the **first** significant digit of the inch-pound value (6). Therefore the number of significant digits to be retained in the converted value is the **same** as that for the original value (3), and the result is 97.4 km.

Similarly, in converting 11 miles to kilometers:

11 miles x 1.609347 = **1**7.70281 km

The **first** significant digit of the metric value (1) is **equal to** the **first** significant digit of the inch-pound value (1). Therefore the number of significant digits to be retained in the converted value is the **same** as that for the original value (2), and the result is 18 km.

(ii) If the **first** significant digit of the converted value is **smaller** than the **first** significant digit of the original value, round to **one more** significant digit.

Example: In converting 66 miles to kilometers, first multiply the inch-pound value by the conversion factor:

66 miles x 1.609347 = **1**06.2169 km

The **first** significant digit of the metric value (1) is **smaller** than the **first** significant digit of the inch-pound value (6). Therefore the number of significant digits to be retained in the converted value should be **one more** than that for the original value (3), and the result is 106 km.

---

[8]   Note that this procedure is the same whether converting from inch-pound to SI or from SI to inch-pound units.

Similarly, in converting 8 feet to meters:

8 feet x 0.3048 = **2**.438400 m

The **first** significant digit of the metric value (2) is **smaller** than the **first** significant digit of the inch-pound value (8). Therefore the number of significant digits to be retained in the converted value should be **one** more than that for the original value (2), and the result is 2.4 m.

4.4.1.2   Rounding Practices Used for Packaged Goods in the Commercial Marketplace

Manufacturers of packaged goods sold in the commercial marketplace are required under either federal or state laws to accurately declare the net quantity of contents of their packages. These quantity declarations are based on the accuracy of packaging machinery and take into account unavoidable deviations in the packaging process. Both federal and state regulations allow manufacturers or packagers to round converted values down to avoid overstating the net quantity of contents declared on package labels.[9] When officials verify the accuracy of multiple quantity declarations, they determine which of the declarations represent the largest net quantity and verify the accuracy of that value.

4.4.1.3   Temperature Rounding

Temperature is usually expressed in degrees Fahrenheit as whole numbers and should be converted to the nearest 0.5 degree Celsius. This is because the magnitude of a degree Celsius (°C) is approximately twice the size of a degree Fahrenheit, and rounding to the nearest Celsius would reduce the precision of the original measurement. As with other quantities, the number of significant digits to retain will depend upon the implied accuracy of the original temperature.

5   DETAILED REQUIREMENTS AND CONVERSION FACTORS

This section gives detailed requirements for the selection of units. The subsections list conversion factors to the appropriately sized metric unit, either an SI unit with appropriate prefix or a non-SI unit that is accepted for use with SI. Government agencies and industry may develop supplemental lists of accepted units applicable to their special fields. Such supplemental lists should be consistent with this document and users should provide their equivalents in SI units unless the quantity being measured cannot be measured in combinations of base or derived SI units (e.g., Rockwell hardness and Richter scale values).

> **Other "Derived Quantities."** It is not practical to list all quantities, but others not listed can be readily derived using the conversion factors given. For example, to convert from inches per second to centimeters per second, multiply by 2.54; to convert from Btu per pound to kilojoules per kilogram, multiply by (1.055 056)/(0.453 592 37) or 2.326 000 3.

> **Note on Mixed Units and Fractions.** Mixed units, which are commonly used with inch-pound units, are not used in metric practice. Thus, while a distance may be given in inch-pound units as 27 feet 5 inches, metric practice shows a length as 3.45 m rather than 3 m, 45 cm. Binary fractions (such as 1/2 or 3/8) are not used with metric units. For example, a person's weight is given as 70.5 kg, not 70-1/2 kg.

The preferred units for various quantities are grouped in subsections as follows: Space and Time, Mechanics, Heat, Electricity and Magnetism, Light, and Radiology.

The tables are presented as follows:

To Convert From	To	Multiply By
Foot	meter (m)	0.3048

---

[9]   For a more detailed discussion, refer to NIST Handbook 130 – *Uniform Laws and Regulations in the area of legal metrology ...* at *http://www.nist.gov/owm* on the Internet

The first column, labeled **To Convert from**, lists inch-pound and other units commonly used to express the quantities; the second column, labeled **To**, gives SI units or other preferred units; and the third column, labeled **Multiply By**, gives the conversion factors (generally to seven significant digits) by which the numerical value in **To Convert From** units must be multiplied to obtain the numerical value in SI units. Conversion factors, in the **Multiply By** column, that are exact conversion values are noted in **bold** type. To convert values expressed in SI unit to the other unit divide the SI unit by the value in the **Multiply By** column.

The conversion factors are:

Section	To Convert From	To	Multiply By
5.1	**Quantities of Space and Time**		
5.1.1	**Plane angle**[10]		
	Radian	degree arc	57.29578
5.1.2	**Solid angle**[11]		
5.1.3	**Length**		
	angstrom	nanometer (nm)	**0.1**
	Fathom	meter (m)	1.828 804
	foot (ft)	meter (m)	**0.304 8**
	foot [U.S. survey][12]	meter (m)	0.304 800 6
	inch (in)	centimeter (cm)	**2.54**
	inch (in)	millimeter (mm)	**25.4**
	microinch (μin)	micrometer (μm)	**0.025 4**
	mil (0.001 inch)	millimeter (mm)	**0.025 4**
	mil (0.001 inch)	micrometer (μm)	**25.4**
	yard (yd)	meter (m)	**0.914 4**
	mile, international (5280 ft) (mi)	kilometer (km)	1.609 344
	nautical mile[13]	kilometer (km)	**1.852**
	point (printer's)	millimeter (mm)	0.351 46
	pica	millimeter (mm)	4.217 5

---

[10] No change in inch-pound usage is required for plane angle units. The **radian**, which is the SI unit, is most frequently used in scientific or technical work and in forming derived units. Use of the degree and its decimal fractions is permissible. Use of the minute and second is discouraged except for specialized fields such as cartography

[11] No change in inch-pound usage is required for solid angle units. The **steradian**, which is the only unit commonly used to express solid angle, is an SI unit.

[12] In 1893 the U.S. foot was legally defined as 1200/3937 meters. In 1959 a refinement was made to bring the foot into agreement with the definition used in other countries, i.e., 0.3048 meters. At the same time it was decided that any data in feet derived from and published as a result of geodetic surveys within the U.S. would remain with the old standard, which is named the U.S. survey foot. The new length is shorter by about two parts in a million. The five-digit multipliers given in this standard for acre and acre-foot are correct for either the U.S. survey foot or the foot of 0.304 8 meters exactly. Other lengths, areas, and volumes are based on the foot of 0.304 8 meters.

[13] The nautical mile is an accepted unit for use in navigation.

Section	To Convert From	To	Multiply By
5.1.4	**Area**		
	acre[14]	square meter (m^2)	4 046.873
	acre	hectare[15] (ha)	0.404 687 3
	circular mil	square millimeter (mm^2)	0.000 506 708
	square inch	square centimeter (cm^2)	**6.451 6**
	square inch	square millimeter (mm^2)	**645.16**
	square foot	square meter (m^2)	**0.092 903 04**
	square yard	square meter (m^2)	**0.836 127 36**
	square mile	square kilometer (km^2)	2.589 988
5.1.5	**Volume**		
	acre-foot	cubic meter (m^3)	1 233.489
	barrel, oil[16] (42 U.S. gallons)	cubic meter (m^3)	0.158 987 3
	barrel, oil (42 U.S. gallons)	liter (L)	158.987 3
	cubic yard	cubic meter (m^3)	0.764 555
	cubic foot	cubic meter (m^3)	0.028 316 85
	cubic foot	liter (L)	28.316 85
	board foot	cubic meter (m^3)	0.002 359 737
	register ton[17]	cubic meter (m^3)	2.831 685
	bushel[18]	cubic meter (m^3)	0.035 239 07
	gallon	liter (L)	3.785 412
	quart (liquid)	liter (L)	0.946 352 9
	pint (liquid)	liter (L)	0.473 176 5

---

[14] Based on U. S. survey foot.

[15] The hectare, equal to 10 000 m^2, is accepted for use with SI.

[16] (i) The liter, equal to 0.001 m^3, is accepted for use with SI. (ii) A variety of barrel sizes have been used for other commodities.

[17] The register ton is a unit of volume used to express the capacity of a ship. For example, a 20 000 ton freighter has a capacity of approximately 57 000 m^3, measured in accordance with established procedures.

[18] Agricultural products that are sold by the bushel in the United States are often sold by weight in other countries. There can be a considerable variation in the weight per unit volume due to differences in variety, size, or condition of the commodity, tightness of pack, degree to which the container is heaped, etc. The following conversion factors are used by the U.S. Department of Agriculture for statistical purposes:

Crop	Weight per bushel (kg)
barley	21.8
com, shelled	25.4
oats	14.5
potatoes, soybeans, wheat	27.2

Section	To Convert From	To	Multiply By
	fluid ounce[19]	milliliter (mL)	29.573 53
	cubic inch	cubic centimeter (cm³)	**16.387 064**
5.1.6	**Time[20]**		
5.1.7	**Velocity**		
	foot per second	meter per second (m /s)	**0.304 8**
	mile per hour	kilometer per hour (km/h)	**1.609 344**
	knot[21] (nautical mile per hour)	kilometer per hour (km/h)	**1.852**
5.1.8	**Acceleration**		
	inch per second squared	meter per second squared (m·s⁻²)	**0.025 4**
	foot per second squared	meter per second squared (m·s⁻²)	**0.304 8**
	standard acceleration of gravity (g_n)	meter per second squared (m·s⁻²)	**9.806 65**
5.1.9	**Flow rate**		
	cubic foot per second	cubic meter per second (m³/s)	0.028 316 85
	cubic foot per minute	cubic meter per second (m³/s)	0.000 471 9474
	cubic foot per minute	liter per second (L/s)	0.471 947 4
	cubic yard per minute	liter per second (L/s)	12.742 58
	gallon per minute	liter per second (L/s)	0.063 090 2
	gallon per day	liter per day (L/d)	3.785 412
5.1.10	**Fuel efficiency**		
	mile per gallon[22]	kilometer per liter (km/L)	0.425 143 7
5.2	**Quantities of Mechanics**		
5.2.1	**Mass (weight[23])**		
	ton (long)[24] (2240 lb)	kilogram (kg)	1 016.047
	ton (long)	metric ton (t)	1.016 047

---

[19] In the United States, the cup, tablespoon, and teaspoon are defined as 8, 1/2, and 1/6 fluid ounces, respectively. For practical usage the metric equivalents are 250 mL, 15 mL, and 5 mL.

[20] No change in inch-pound U.S. usage is required for time units. The second is the SI unit of time, but the minute and hour, as well as the day, week, year, etc., are accepted units.

[21] The knot, or nautical mile per hour, is an accepted unit for use in navigation.

[22] Fuel consumption (e.g., liter/kilometer) is the reciprocal of fuel efficiency. Thus, 20 mile/gallon fuel efficiency is equal to 20(0.42514)=8 503 km/L, which is equivalent to a fuel consumption of 1/8.503=0.1176 L/km, or more conveniently 11.76 L/ 100 km.

[23] There is ambiguity in the use of the term "weight" to mean either *force* or *mass*. In general usage, the term "weight" nearly always means *mass* and this is the meaning given the term in U.S. laws and regulations. Where the term is so used, weight is expressed in **kilograms** in SI. In many fields of science and technology the term "weight" is defined as the *force* of gravity acting on an object, i.e., as the product of the *mass* of the object and the local acceleration of gravity. Where weight is so defined, it is expressed in **newtons** in SI.

[24] The metric ton (referred to as "tonne" in many countries), equal to 1000 kg, is accepted for use with SI.

Section	To Convert From	To	Multiply By
	ton (short) (2000 lb)	kilogram (kg)	**907.184 74**
	ton (short)	metric ton (t)	**0.907 184 74**
	slug	kilogram (kg)	14.593 9
	pound (avoirdupois)	kilogram (kg)	**0.453 592 37**
	ounce (troy)	gram (g)	31.103 48
	ounce (avoirdupois)	gram (g)	28.349 52
	grain	milligram (mg)	**64.798 91**
5.2.2	**Moment of mass**		
	pound foot	kilogram meter (kg · m)	0.138 255
5.2.3	**Density**		
	ton (2 000 lb ([short]) per cubic yard	kilogram per cubic meter (kg /m^3)	1 186. 553
		metric ton per cubic meter (t /m^3)	1.186 553
	pound per cubic foot	kilogram per cubic meter (kg /m^3)	16.018 46
5.2.4	**Concentration (mass)**		
	pound per gallon	gram per liter (g /L)	119.826 4
	ounce (avoirdupois) per gallon	gram per liter (g /L)	7.489 152
5.2.5	**Momentum**		
	pound foot per second	kilogram meter per second (kg · m /s)	0.138 255 0
5.2.6	**Moment of inertia**		
	pound square foot	kilogram square meter (kg · m^2)	0.042 140 11
5.2.7	**Force**		
	pound-force	newton (N)	4.448 222
	poundal	newton (N)	0.138 255 0
5.2.8	**Moment of force, torque**		
	pound-force foot	newton meter (N · m)	1.355 818
	pound-force inch	newton meter (N · m)	0.112 984 8
5.2.9	**Pressure, stress**		
	standard atmosphere[25]	kilopascal (kPa)	**101.325**

---

[25] The SI unit for pressure and stress is the pascal, which is equal to the newton per square meter. This unit, its multiple, and submultiples are preferred for all applications.

Section	To Convert From	To	Multiply By
	bar[26]	kilopascal (kPa)	**100**
	millibar	kilopascal (kPa)	**0.1**
	pound-force per square inch (psi)	kilopascal (kPa)	6.894 757
	kilopound-force per square inch	megapascal (MPa)	6.894 757
	pound-force per square foot	kilopascal (kPa)	0.047 880 26
	inch of mercury[26] (32 °F)	kilopascal (kPa)	3.386 38
	foot of water[26] (39.2 °F)	kilopascal (kPa)	2.988 98
	inch of water[26] (39.2 °F)	kilopascal (kPa)	0.249 082
	millimeter of mercury[27] (32 °F)	kilopascal kPa)	0.133 322 4
	torr (Torr)	pascal (Pa)	133.322 4
5.2.10	**Viscosity (dynamic)**		
	centipoise	millipascal second (mPa · s)	**1**
5.2.11	**Viscosity (kinematic)**		
	centistokes	square millimeter per second (mm^2/s)	**1**
5.2.12	**Energy, work, heat**		
	kilowatthour[28]	megajoule (MJ)	**3.6**
	calorie[29] (as used in physics)	joule (J)	**4.184**
	calorie[30] (as used in nutrition)	kilojoule (kJ)	**4.184**
	Btu[31]	kilojoule (kJ)	1.055 056
	therm (U.S.)	megajoule (MJ)	**105.480 4**
	horsepower hour	megajoule (MJ)	2.684 520
	foot pound-force	joule (J)	1.355 818

---

[26] The bar and its submultiples are accepted for limited use in meteorology only. It is not accepted for use in the U.S. for other applications, e.g., as the unit of fluid pressure in pipes and containers. The appropriate SI multiples, e.g., **kilopascal** or **megapascal**, should be used instead.

[27] The actual pressure corresponding to the height of a vertical column of fluid depends upon the local acceleration of gravity and the density of the fluid, which in turn depends upon the temperature. The conversion factors given here are conventional values adopted by the International Organization for Standardization (ISO).

[28] The kilowatthour is accepted as a unit of electrical energy only. The SI unit of energy, the **joule**, which is equal to the newton meter or the watt second, is recommended for all applications.

[29] The calorie listed here is the thermochemical calorie. Other values of the calorie have been used.

[30] The calorie used in nutrition is the same as the thermochemical **kilocalorie** or kcal. One food calorie equals about 4,186 J. All use of the calorie is deprecated.

[31] The British Thermal Unit (Btu) used in this standard is the International Table Btu (Btu$_{IT}$) adopted by the Fifth International Conference on Properties of Steam, London, 1956.

Section	To Convert From	To	Multiply By
5.2.13	**Power**[32]		
	ton, refrigeration (12 000 Btu/h)	kilowatt (kW)	3.516 853
	Btu per second[31]	kilowatt (kW)	1.055 056
	Btu per hour[31]	watt (W)	0.293 071 1
	horsepower (550 foot pounds-force per second)	watt (W)	745.699 9
	horsepower, electric	watt (W)	**746**
	foot pound-force per second	watt (W)	1.355 818
5.3	**Quantities of Heat**		
5.3.1	**Temperature**[33]		
5.3.2	**Linear expansion coefficient**		
	reciprocal degree Fahrenheit	reciprocal kelvin (K^{-1})	**1.8**
	reciprocal degree Fahrenheit	reciprocal degree Celsius $(°C^{-1})$	**1.8**
5.3.3	**Heat**[34]		
5.3.4	**Heat flow rate**[35]		
5.3.5	**Thermal conductivity**		
	Btu inch per hour square foot degree Fahrenheit	watt per meter kelvin $[W / (m \cdot K)]$	0.144 227 9
5.3.6	**Coefficient of heat transfer**		
	Btu per hour square foot degree Fahrenheit	watt per square meter kelvin $[W / (m^2 \cdot K)]$	5.678 263
5.3.7	**Heat capacity**		
	Btu per degree Fahrenheit	kilojoule per kelvin (kJ/K)	1.899 101
5.3.8	**Specific heat capacity**		
	Btu per pound degree Fahrenheit	kilojoule per kilogram kelvin $[kJ/(kg \cdot K)]$	**4.186 8**
5.3.9	**Entropy**		
	Btu per degree Rankine	kilojoule per kelvin (kJ/K)	1.899 101
5.3.10	**Specific entropy**		

[32] NOTE: Power is the rate of energy transfer. The SI unit for all forms of power—mechanical, electrical, and heat flow rate—is the **watt**.

[33] The SI unit for temperature is the **degree Celsius** (C) or the kelvin (K). In inch-pound units temperature is expressed in degrees Fahrenheit. The formula for converting temperature is:

$$t_C = (t_F - 32) / 1.8$$

The SI unit for thermodynamic temperature T_K is the kelvin (K). The Celsius temperature is defined by the equation: $t_C = T_K - 273.15$ K. The inch-pound unit for thermodynamic temperature is the degree Rankine. The formula for converting degree Rankine to thermodynamic temperature is: $T_K = T_R / 1.8$.

A temperature interval may be expressed in SI either in kelvin or in degrees Celsius, as convenient. The formula for converting a temperature interval Δt in degrees Fahrenheit into SI is:

$$\Delta t_K = \Delta t_C = \Delta t_F / 1.8.$$

[34] Heat is a form of energy. See 5.3.7.

[35] Heat flow rate is a form of power. See 5.2.12.

Section	To Convert From	To	Multiply By
	Btu per pound degree Rankine	kilojoule per kilogram kelvin [kJ/(kg · K)]	**4.186 8**
5.3.11	**Specific internal energy**		
	Btu per pound	kilojoule per kilogram (kJ/kg)	**2.326**
5.4	**Quantities of Electricity and Magnetism**[36]		
5.4.1	**Magnetic field strength**		
	oersted	ampere per meter (A/m)	79.577 47
5.4.2	**Magnetic flux**		
	maxwell	nanoweber (nWb)	**10**
5.4.3	**Magnetic flux density**		
	gauss	millitesla (mT)	**0.1**
5.4.4	**Electric charge**		
	ampere hour	coulomb (C)	**3 600**
5.4.5	**Resistivity**		
	ohm circular mil per foot	nanoohm meter (nΩ · m)	1.662 426
5.4.6	**Conductivity**		
	mho per centimeter	siemens per meter (S/m)	**100**
5.5	**Quantities of Light and Related Electromagnetic Radiation**[37]		
5.5.1	**Wavelength**		
	ångström	nanometer (nm)	**0.1**
5.5.2	**Luminance**		
	lambert (L)	candela per square meter (cd/m^2)	3 183.099
	candela per square inch	candela per square meter (cd /m^2)	1 550.003
	footlambert	candela per square meter (cd /m^2)	3.426 259
5.5.3	**Luminous exitance**		
	lumen per square foot	lux (lx)	10.763 91
	phot	lux (lx)	**10 000**
5.5.4	**Illuminance**		
	footcandle	lux (lx)	10.763 91
5.6	**Quantities of Radiology**		

---

[36] The common electrical units **ampere** (A), **volt** (V), **ohm** (Ω), **siemens** (S), **coulomb** (C), **farad** (F), **henry** (H), **weber** (Wb), and **tesla** (T) are SI units that are already in use in the United States. The various Centimeter-Gram-Second (CGS) units shall no longer be used.

[37] No change is required for the following quantities: radiant intensity, watt per steradian (W/sr); radiance, watt per steradian square meter (W/[sr · m^2]); irradiance, watt per square meter (W/m^2); luminous intensity, candela (cd); luminous flux, lumen (lm); and quantity of light, lumen second (lm · s).

Section	To Convert From	To	Multiply By
5.6.1	**Activity (of a radionuclide)**		
	Curie	megabecquerel (MBq)	**37 000**
5.6.2	**Absorbed dose**		
	Rad	gray (Gy)	**0.01**
	Rad	centigray (cGy)	**1**
5.6.3	**Dose equivalent**		
	Rem	sievert (Sv)	**0.01**
	Rem	millisievert (mSv)	**10**
	Millirem	millisievert (mSv)	**0.01**
	Millirem	microsievert (µSv)	**10**
5.6.4	**Exposure (x and gamma rays)**		
	roentgen	coulomb per kilogram (C/kg)	**0.000 258**

6   DOCUMENT SOURCES

Copies of SI 10™ are available from:

American Society for Testing Materials International (ASTM), 100 Barr Harbor Drive, West Conshohocken, PA 19428-2959. Phone: 610-832-9585, Fax: 610-832-9555, or at *http://www.astm.org*

NIST publications and Federal Standard 376B are available on the Internet at:

http://www.nist.gov/metric

For print copies of NIST SP 330, NIST SP 811 or NIST SP 814 or other assistance please contact:

Elizabeth J. Gentry, National Institute of Standards and Technology, Weights and Measures Division, Laws and Metric Group, Mail Stop 2600, Gaithersburg, Maryland 20899-2600. Phone: 301-975-3690, FAX: 301-926-0647, or e-mail: *TheSI@nist.gov*.

7   BIBLIOGRAPHY

1. IEEE, *American National Standard for Use of the International System of Units (SI): The Modern Metric System,* IEEE/ASTM SI 10™ (2002).

2. ASTM, IEEE/ASTM-SI-10 *Standard for Use of the International System of Units (SI): The Modern Metric System.* This document replaces ASTM E380 and ANSI/IEEE Standard 268-1992.

3. *The International System of Units (SI),* (2001) National Institute of Standards and Technology (NIST) Special Publication 330.

4. *Guide for the Use of the International System of Units, The Modernized Metric System,* (1995) NIST Special Publication 811.

5. *Interpretation of the SI and Metric Conversion Policy for Federal Agencies,* NIST Special Publication 814, 1998 edition, which includes:

> *Metric System of Measurement; Interpretation of the International System of Units for the United States,* (63 F.R. 40334, July 28, 1998);

> *Metric Conversion Policy for Federal Agencies,* (56 F.R. 160, January 2, 1991); and

> *Metric Usage in Federal Government Programs,* Executive Order 12770 of July 25,1991 (56 FR 35801, July 29, 1991).

6. Federal Standard 376B "*Preferred Metric Units for General Use by the Federal Government*" (January 27, 1993).

ALPHABETICAL INDEX

CPSIA information can be obtained
at www.ICGtesting.com
Printed in the USA
LVOW03s1606180416

484152LV00013B/349/P